Zoom In on

In the Sky

Snow

Andrea Rivera

abdopublishing.com

Published by Abdo Zoom™, PO Box 398166, Minneapolis, Minnesota 55439. Copyright © 2017 by Abdo Consulting Group, Inc. International copyrights reserved in all countries. No part of this book may be reproduced in any form without written permission from the publisher. Abdo Zoom™ is a trademark and logo of Abdo Consulting Group, Inc.

Printed in the United States of America, North Mankato, Minnesota
102016
012017

THIS BOOK CONTAINS
RECYCLED MATERIALS

Cover Photo: Shutterstock Images
Interior Photos: Shutterstock Images, 1, 4–5, 18, 19; Toth Gabor Cyula/iStockphoto, 5; Mike Richter/Shutterstock Images, 6; Iurii Davydov/Shutterstock Images, 7; NASA, 8, 9; iStockphoto, 10, 13; Trudy Wilkerson/Shutterstock Images, 11; Francesco de Marco/Shutterstock Images, 12; Kyodo/AP Images, 14–15; Вадим Черенко/iStockphoto, 16–17, 17; Matt Ragen/Shutterstock Images, 21

Editor: Emily Temple
Series Designer: Madeline Berger
Art Direction: Dorothy Toth

Publisher's Cataloging-in-Publication Data
Names: Rivera, Andrea, author.
Title: Snow / by Andrea Rivera.
Description: Minneapolis, MN : Abdo Zoom, 2017. | Series: In the sky |
    Includes bibliographical references and index.
Identifiers: LCCN 2016948921 | ISBN 9781680799347 (lib. bdg.) |
    ISBN 9781624025204 (ebook) | ISBN 9781624025761 (Read-to-me ebook)
Subjects: LCSH: Snow--Juvenile literature.
Classification: DDC 551.57/84-dc23
LC record available at http://lccn.loc.gov/2016948921

Table of Contents

Science

Snow comes from clouds.

Water in the air freezes.
It forms ice crystals.
The crystals grow.

5

The crystals fall from the cloud. They bump into each other.

They stick together.
This forms snowflakes.

Scientists use satellites
to track snow.

Satellites take pictures of Earth. The pictures show which way snow clouds are moving. Scientists can warn people a snowstorm is coming.

In 1921 in Colorado more than 6 feet (1.8 m) of snow fell in a day. The snow piled up to the top of a house's door.

This was the record for the most snow in the shortest time.

Engineering

Snowshoes help people walk in
snow. They are wide and long.

They spread a person's weight
over more snow. This makes less
pressure on the snow. It keeps the
person from sinking in. 13

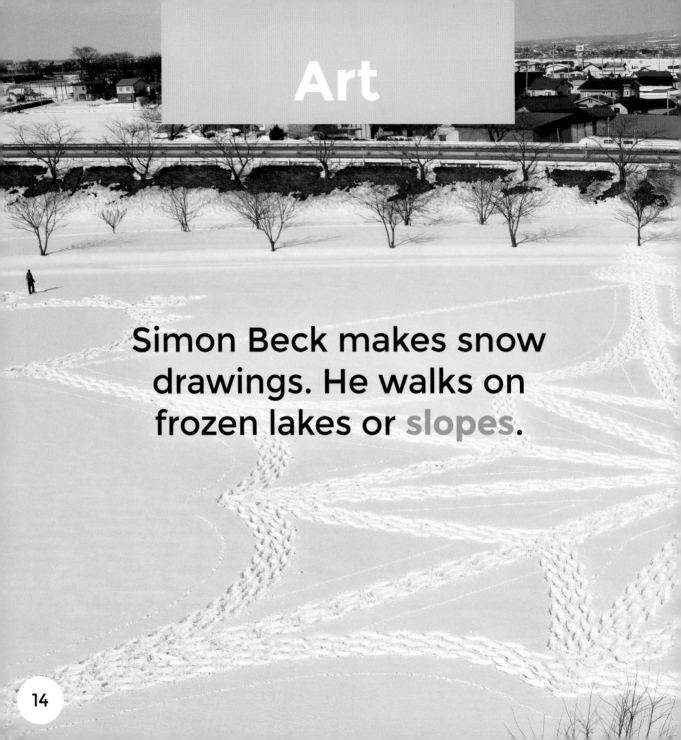

Art

Simon Beck makes snow drawings. He walks on frozen lakes or slopes.

His tracks make a
pattern. From above
it looks like a picture.

Math

Most snowflakes have six sides. But no two snowflakes are the same.

Some have six branches.

Some have six flat sides.
They look like hexagons.

Others are long and
skinny like pencils.

Key Stats

- The ice crystals in snow are tiny. One snowflake might be made of 100 ice crystals.

- Most snowflakes fall 36 inches (91 cm) per second. That is as fast as a car driving in a parking lot.

- Paradise Ranger Station in Washington is one of Earth's snowiest places. It can get 83 feet (25 m) of snow in one year.

21

Glossary

hexagon - a shape with six straight sides.

ice crystal - tiny pieces of ice that can grow into snowflakes.

pressure - pressing or pushing against something.

satellite - a device or object that orbits the earth.

slope - an area of land on the side of a mountain that is used for skiing.

Booklinks

For more information
on snow, please visit
booklinks.abdopublishing.com

Zoom In on STEAM!

Learn even more with the Abdo Zoom
STEAM database. Check out
abdozoom.com for more information.

Index